Taipan

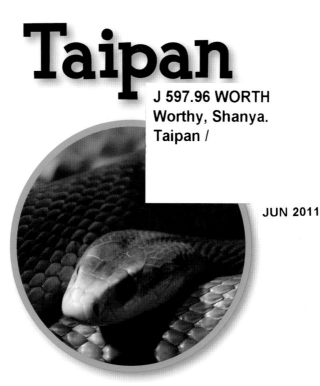

By Shanya Worthy

Gareth Stevens

Please visit our Web site, www.garethstevens.com. For a free color catalog of all our high-quality books, call toll free 1-800-542-2595 or fax 1-877-542-2596.

Library of Congress Cataloging-in-Publication Data

Worthy, Shanya.
Taipan / Shanya Worthy.
    p. cm. — (Killer snakes)
Includes index.
ISBN 978-1-4339-4566-3 (pbk.)
ISBN 978-1-4339-4567-0 (6-pack)
ISBN 978-1-4339-4565-6 (library binding)
1. Oxyuranus—Juvenile literature. I. Title.
QL666.O64W58 2010
597.96'4—dc22

                                    2010030694

First Edition

Published in 2011 by
Gareth Stevens Publishing
111 East 14th Street, Suite 349
New York, NY 10003

Copyright © 2011 Gareth Stevens Publishing

Designer: Michael J. Flynn
Editor: Greg Roza

Photo credits: Cover, pp. 1, (2–4, 6–8, 10, 12, 14, 16, 18, 20–24 snake skin texture), 5, 9, 17 Shutterstock.com; pp. 6–7, 19 Brooke Watnall/National Geographic/Getty Images; p. 11 DEA/C.DANI-I.JESKE/De Agostini Picture Library/Getty Images; p. 13 Nicole Duplaix/National Geographic/Getty Images; p. 15 Jason Edwards/National Geographic/Getty Images; p. 21 iStockphoto.com.

Printed in the United States of America

CPSIA compliance information: Batch #CW11GS: For further information contact Gareth Stevens, New York, New York at 1-800-542-2595.

Contents

Boldface words appear in the glossary.

Types of Taipans

Three kinds of taipans live in Australia and New Guinea. Inland taipans live in the deserts of central Australia. Coastal taipans live along the northern coast of Australia and the southern coast of New Guinea. The Central Ranges taipan was just discovered in 2006!

KEY

coastal taipan

inland taipan

Central Ranges taipan

New Guinea

Australia

5

Taipan Bodies

The coastal taipan is the longest. Most grow to about 6 to 8 feet (1.8 to 2.4 m). They can be black, gray, or brown. Inland taipans are smaller. Most grow to about 5 feet (1.5 m) long. They are mostly brown or black.

coastal taipan

7

The Inland Taipan

The inland taipan lives in the desert where there are very few plants. It hides in cracks and under rocks. The taipan's **scales** are often darker in winter than in summer. This allows the taipan to take in more heat from the sun in cold weather.

inland taipan

9

Laying Eggs

Female inland taipans lay 12 to 20 eggs at one time. They lay them in an animal den or a crack in the ground. Then they leave the eggs. The baby taipans break out of the eggs about 2 months later.

11

Deadly!

All taipans are deadly snakes. They use **venom** to kill. The venom of the inland taipan is the strongest of any land snake on Earth. Just one bite has enough venom to kill 100 people! The venom can cause the taipan's **prey** to bleed to death.

13

Like most snakes, taipans have sharp teeth called fangs. They use their fangs to **inject** their venom into other animals. They do this to catch prey. They also do it to chase away enemies. Taipans sometimes bite people, but only when they're scared or trapped.

15

Hungry?

Taipans eat birds, lizards, and **rodents**. Inland taipans mainly like to eat rats. Taipans hunt in the morning when it's cooler. During really hot weather, taipans hunt at night. A taipan **attacks** so quickly the prey often doesn't even see it!

A taipan bite injects venom into its prey. Once a taipan bites its prey, it lets go and waits for the prey to die. The venom is strong and works fast. Once the prey is dead, the taipan eats it whole!

Taipans and People

Taipans don't commonly attack people. However, they may attack if a person scares them or tries to catch them. Someone who is bitten by a taipan must take a drug called antivenin. This drug stops the venom from working. Without antivenin, the person will die.

Snake Facts
Inland Taipan

Length	about 5 feet (1.5 m) long
Where It Lives	central desert of Australia
How Many Eggs a Female Lays	12 to 20 at one time
Favorite Food	rats
Killer Fact	A single bite from an inland taipan has enough venom to kill 100 adult people or 250,000 mice!

Glossary

attack: to try to harm someone or something

inject: to use sharp teeth to force venom into an animal's body

prey: an animal hunted by other animals for food

rodent: a small, furry animal with large front teeth, such as a mouse or rat

scale: one of the plates that cover a snake's body

venom: something a snake makes in its body that can harm other animals

For More Information

Books

Jenkins, Jennifer Meghan. *The 10 Deadliest Snakes.* Oakville, ON, Canada: Rubicon Publishers, 2007.

Wechsler, Doug. *Taipans.* New York, NY: PowerKids Press, 2001.

Web Sites

Corwin's Quest: Inland Taipan

animal.discovery.com/videos/corwins-quest-inland-taipan.html

Snake expert Jeff Corwin tracks down an inland taipan.

Wild Recon: Coastal Taipan Venom

animal.discovery.com/videos/wild-recon-coastal-taipan-venom.html

Donald Schultz, host of Wild Recon, collects venom from a coastal taipan.

Index